The Twilight Realm

The Undead

Please visit our website, **www.garethstevens.com**. For a free color catalog of all our high-quality books, call toll free 1-800-542-2595 or fax 1-877-542-2596.

Library of Congress Cataloging-in-Publication Data

Pipe, Jim, 1966-
 The undead / Jim Pipe.
    p. cm. — (The twilight realm)
 Includes bibliographical references (p.   ) and index.
 ISBN 978-1-4339-8760-1 (pbk.)
 ISBN 978-1-4339-8761-8 (6-pack)
 ISBN 978-1-4339-8759-5 (library binding)
 1. Vampires—Juvenile literature. I. Title.
 BF1556.P56 2013
 398'.45—dc23

                                2012038519

Published in 2013 by
Gareth Stevens Publishing
111 East 14th Street, Suite 349
New York, NY 10003

© 2013 Gareth Stevens Publishing

Produced for Gareth Stevens by Wayland a division of Hachette Children's Books
a Hachette UK company
www.hachette.co.uk

Editor: Paul Manning
Designer: Paul Manning

Picture Credits

18, 19, 24, 25, Wikimedia Commons. All other images © Shutterstock. www.bergoiata.org.

Printed in the United States of America

CPSIA compliance information: Batch CW13GS: For further information contact Gareth Stevens,
New York, New York at 1-800-542-2595.

The Twilight Realm

The Undead

Jim Pipe

Gareth Stevens
Publishing

Contents

Vampire Alert!

It's night. Outside your window, all is silent. But in their secret hiding places, vampires are stirring. Soon their craving for blood will become irresistible. The Undead are about to seek another innocent victim…

▶ *Forget tall Eastern European gents in shiny black capes and suits. Centuries of cunning have enabled vampires to live and move among human beings virtually undetected. So how do you spot the telltale signs?*

Eyes: glowing with menace

Pale, greenish complexion

Vicious fangs, filed to a point for easy feeding

Foul breath

ales of the Undead are told by people in countries all over the world. All the stories agree on one thing: vampires are the restless souls of the dead that prey on the living. At night, while the world sleeps, they roam the streets, hunting for victims.

For all their supernatural powers, vampires have a weakness: a desperate thirst for human blood. Beware the flashing eyes and seductive smile. They want nothing more than to sink their fangs deep into your neck. One bite and you too will join the Undead – forever!

▲ *Spooky graveyards and dark alleys are the traditional hunting grounds for vampires. You have been warned!*

"Yes, vampires live forever. How often do we mortals dream of such a thing? But imagine the countless nights of slaughter. For without blood, a vampire's body will crumble to dust!"

from The Tireless Vampire Hunter by Hugo Van Helsing

All in the Mind?

Most people would say that vampires belong firmly to the world of superstition. But in some parts of the world, belief in vampires remains strong. During late 2002 and early 2003, hysteria about mysterious blood-sucking attacks swept through the African country of Malawi. Mobs stoned one person to death and attacked a leading politician, claiming that the government was in league with vampires.

▲ *Beautiful by day, the legendary Loogaroo vampire of the Caribbean sheds her skin at night and prowls local villages, slaking her thirst on the blood of young men.*

Night Attack!

A teenage boy walks home from a night out with his friends. It's a dark, moonless night, and he's already spooked by the flickering shadows and the quiet patter of footsteps behind him…

▼ *It's not just a vampire's fangs that a victim needs to watch out for. Some vampires file their nails to a sharp point to dig into the flesh of their victims.*

Suddenly, as he enters a narrow alley, the vampire is upon him, his eyes blazing like burning coals in the darkness. Crazed by bloodlust, the attacker is far faster and stronger than his victim. Though the boy puts up a brave fight, he is soon helpless in the vampire's steely grip.

Just then comes the sound of footsteps approaching – a group of partygoers returning home. The vampire makes a swift decision and vanishes into the night as quickly as he appeared. If the boy ever tells of his lucky escape, who will believe him?

▲ Vampire lore warns against staring into the cold, glassy eyes of the Undead. Mesmerized by the vampire's hypnotic powers, victims are powerless to resist.

"The vampire virus has been known to create strange mutations. In Bulgaria, the Ubour uses a forked tongue to pierce its victim's neck rather than fangs."

from Le Chasseur de Vampires by Vincent Lepique

Kiss of Death

Fangs bared and fingers clasped around the victim's neck is the vampire's classic attack mode. But not all vampires go for the neck. In some stories, vampires suck on blood pumping near the heart. Others chomp between the eyes or suck blood from the feet. The vampires of Eastern European folklore hugged their victims (cows and pigs) to death, then slurped on their blood afterwards.

Becoming a Vampire

Many people tease their friends that the strange marks on their neck mean they'll turn into vampires. But if you believe the stories, it's no laughing matter.

According to legend, it took three bites from the Undead to turn a victim into a vampire. In later stories, witches and werewolves became vampires when they died, as did people who were not properly buried (such as upside down).

More recent vampire theory is less about superstition and more about biology – but just as chilling. A single bite from a vampire is said to infect the victim with a virus. This makes vampire hunting all the more dangerous: a single nick from a vampire's jagged fingernails is enough to infect you. It gets worse. For all the wonders of modern medicine, there is no known antidote to the vampire virus…

► In folktales, the moon is often linked to strange events. A person born on the night of a new moon will change from human to vampire as the moon becomes full.

Natural–Born Vampires

Long ago, people who were cruel, violent, or deceitful were often thought to return from the grave as vampires. But people could also become vampires through no fault of their own. In Slavic countries where most people had dark hair and dark eyes, any child who was born blue-eyed or redheaded was believed to turn into a vampire after they died!

"In many ways, a vampyre's body is similar to our own. But by changing the chemical balance in the brain, the virus makes enormous changes to behaviour, senses and muscle."

from Anatomy of A Vampyre by Dr. Cornelius Sextus

In modern lore, the process of becoming a vampire, or "turning," has three stages:

1. Infection

A few hours after being bitten, the victim develops a fever, a headache, and a rash on their skin as their body tries to battle the infection.

2. Not Dead but Undead

The victim falls into a coma. (In the past, coma victims were sometimes buried alive by mistake. Those who wake up later in their coffin were often found to have made desperate efforts to escape.)

3. Reborn a Vampire

A day or so later, the victim awakes. The transformation is complete. By nightfall, driven wild by the lust for human blood, they will seek out their first victim.

▶ *It's said that in the final stage of the transformation, the victim hungrily laps up the blood of the master vampire. Ugh!*

Vampire Powers

The decision to confront a vampire should not be taken lightly. The Undead are armed with an array of supernatural powers to help them in their battle against the living.

Super Senses

Unless they are asleep or feeding, you have little or no chance of sneaking up on vampires unnoticed. The vampire virus gives them the nose of a bloodhound, the sharp ears of a wolf, and the night vision of a cat.

But a vampire's super senses can be used against them. Bright lights, powerful smells, and extremely loud noises are all said to startle and drive them off.

"For all his might, Dracula himself was aided by a gang of gypsies who tended to his coffins and guarded him while he slept. His manservant, Renfield, was so in fear of Dracula, he obeyed his every command."

from The Lord of Darkness by Bela Barbu

While the powers described below are frightening enough, in folklore, powerful vampires can control wind and rain. Others make great swarms of rats or locusts attack their enemies. It's said Dracula could turn into a green mist to give vampire hunters the slip or creep unseen into his victims' homes.

▼ *Legends tell of master vampires that can transform, or "shape-shift," themselves into hideous human-sized bats or monstrous, slavering wolves.*

Superhuman Strength

The "older" the vampire, the stronger it grows. A well-fed vampire never tires or ages, and its body can recover in seconds from an ordinary bullet or knife wound. Vampires are incredibly fast and agile, too, scampering up walls and scuttling across ceilings like giant spiders.

Mind Control

It's said that vampires need only to catch your gaze for a few seconds to have complete control of your mind. That's why their victims often have no memory of being attacked.

Once bitten, a single glance from a vampire can bring its victim totally under its command. As it feasts on their blood, it drains away their energy, their beauty – and their soul.

Protect and Survive

Do strange shadows flit past your window at night? Do you hear strange screeching noises? Could there be a vampire in your neighborhood?

▲ Strong-smelling garlic was widely believed to repel vampires, who were said to have sensitive noses.

Fear not. Vampire lore is full of suggestions about how to protect yourself. Early vampire hunters relied on garlic and religious symbols such as crosses and holy water to defend themselves against their fanged foes. They also trusted that vampires would recoil in horror at the sound of church bells or the sign of the cross.

The Roma people of central and eastern Europe wore charms such as tigers' teeth and iron rings set with pearls. They also believed that socks stolen from a dead person were a powerful way to ward off vampires.

► Some vampire stories claim that the Undead back away from crosses as they are an ancient symbol of light.

According to today's vampire experts, this is all hocus-pocus. Their advice is simple: make use of what is known. Many vampires avoid direct sunlight, so you are generally safe during the day. At night, trust only your instincts and your weapons.

▶ *Spitting fiercely, a vampire shrinks in terror at the sign of the cross.*

Mirror, Mirror

If you're looking out for vampires, don't forget the theory that they cast no shadow. Having no soul, they were once thought to cast no reflection in a mirror either. Recent vampire lore refutes this, possibly because modern mirrors are no longer made of polished silver, to which vampires reacted badly.

Wolfsbane and Wild Roses

In parts of eastern Germany, superstitious people placed sprigs of wolfsbane under babies' cribs and mattresses to keep away vampires. Wild roses or thorns were also strung around the outside of coffins to discourage vampires from leaving their grave.

To Kill a Vampire

When faced by a creature as hideous as this, few vampire hunters would hesitate before slaying their foe. If they did, they wouldn't last long.

◀ *This vampire looks old and frail, but don't be fooled. Centuries-old vampires are still dangerous enemies.*

Tracking down a vampire is hard enough, but how do you kill a creature that's already dead? In old stories, vampire hunters led their horse around until it got spooked, a sure sign that a vampire den was close by. To put the Undead out of action, they then placed a bulb of garlic in its mouth or a cross under its chin. A more permanent solution was to drive a wooden stake through the vampire's heart, cut off its head, and burn the body.

By all accounts, vampires today are even tougher to exterminate. Even at rest, they remain on the alert. Today's vampire hunters won't get close enough to use a wooden stake without years of martial arts training and plenty of weaponry on hand. Lone vampires are deadly enough, but some stories describe vampires hunting in packs of as many as a dozen.

"The organs were cut out, and one piece after another burnt. Last of all the heart was burnt, and those who attended came near so that the smoke passed over them, and protected them from evil."

from *The Vampire in Romania* by Agnes Murgoci

Death by Silver

In ancient lore, this white, reflective metal, linked to the moon, was also a symbol of purity. In many parts of Eastern Europe, it was believed to have a deadly effect on monsters like vampires and werewolves.

Tiny particles of silver mixed into water have also been used for centuries to stop the spread of all sorts of germs and bacteria, so the modern view is that silver could have a similar effect on the vampire virus.

► Driving a wooden stake into a vampire's heart is not for the squeamish. Apart from the mess, it takes a hefty blow.

Prince of Darkness

Dracula! The name alone sends a shiver down the spine. Look no further if you want to learn about the vampires of the past.

Author Bram Stoker based his vampire on Eastern European folktales, but his creation remains the most famous vampire in the world.

In the story, Count Dracula lures a young Englishman, Jonathan Harker, to his castle in Transylvania by asking him to help him buy property in London. Leaving Harker a prisoner in his lair, he travels to England by ship in boxes filled with earth from his homeland.

Once in England, Dracula sinks his fangs into Lucy, a friend of Harker's fiancée, Mina. Vampire expert Dr. Van Helsing is called in to investigate, but not soon enough to stop Lucy from turning into a vampire.

"My feelings changed to repulsion and terror when I saw him slowly emerge from the window and crawl down the castle wall over the dreadful abyss, with his cloak spreading out around him like great wings."

from the novel Dracula by Bram Stoker

▲ Stoker dreamed up new powers for his blood-sucking hero. Dracula could climb up walls, control the weather, and walk around in daylight without turning to dust.

Van Helsing destroys the undead Lucy with a stake through the heart, then sets out to deal with Dracula. Meanwhile, Harker escapes from Transylvania and joins Van Helsing and a group of friends in the hunt. By finding Dracula's den and destroying most of his coffins, they manage to drive the "Prince of Darkness" out of England.

In the meantime, Dracula has attacked Mina, feeding her with his blood so that she will become a vampire, too. The friends race across Europe and manage to kill Dracula as the sun sets, just in time to save Mina from his clutches.

▲ Working on his novel in the 1890s, Stoker came across a newspaper clipping about South American vampire bats – giving him the idea that Dracula could turn himself into a monstrous bat.

▼ Transylvania is home to the spooky Bran Castle, one of Vlad Dracul's haunts. Bram Stoker used it as the model for Dracula's castle.

The Real Dracula

Prince Dracula was a real person – and just as bloodthirsty as his fictional namesake. On St. Bartholomew's Day 1469, Vlad III of Wallachia, nicknamed Dracul or "dragon," ordered 30,000 enemy prisoners to be impaled on sharp wooden stakes. The prince then set up a picnic table and enjoyed lunch surrounded by this forest of corpses.

19

Vampire Haunts

Back in the mists of time, the Undead were pictured hanging out in remote caves and castles. In modern lore, the vampire menace is all around us: not just in graveyards, but in lonely subways, empty houses, and rotting sewers below the city streets.

▼ *By tradition, vampires slept in coffins filled with earth from the land of their birth. Modern tales suggest they sleep wherever they feel safe.*

The "Cursed Land"?

With its crumbling castles, misty forests, and craggy mountains, Transylvania has long been regarded as the natural home of the Undead. Yet most of the early vampire reports came not from Transylvania, but from countries such as Greece and Serbia. Modern vampire hunters should be on the alert wherever they are. Even Dracula himself moved to London to live among the crowds – an endless supply of victims for the Prince of Darkness!

MORT DU CHOLERA
Certifié par nous Docteur

So where do you start looking? It's said that most vampires have a very bad reaction to sunlight, so a dark den is a must. They also need somewhere to rest during the day, where they're hidden from pesky vampire hunters. No wonder that vampires were mostly thought to live in gloomy graveyards.

That said, there's no reason why vampires have to live in a graveyard. This myth probably comes from gravediggers who claimed to see vampires leaving tombs and coffins. The fresh corpses found here would make easy pickings for a ravenous vampire. Slurp!

Is there a vampire in your area?
• Read your local paper and check out the local history on the Internet.
• Was your town affected by plague?
• Are there any legends of bloodthirsty nobles?

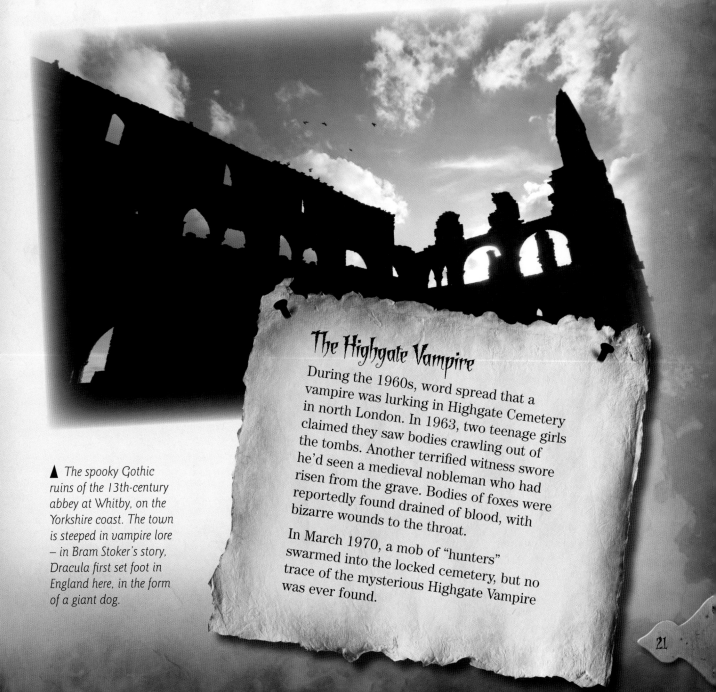

▲ The spooky Gothic ruins of the 13th-century abbey at Whitby, on the Yorkshire coast. The town is steeped in vampire lore – in Bram Stoker's story, Dracula first set foot in England here, in the form of a giant dog.

The Highgate Vampire

During the 1960s, word spread that a vampire was lurking in Highgate Cemetery in north London. In 1963, two teenage girls claimed they saw bodies crawling out of the tombs. Another terrified witness swore he'd seen a medieval nobleman who had risen from the grave. Bodies of foxes were reportedly found drained of blood, with bizarre wounds to the throat.

In March 1970, a mob of "hunters" swarmed into the locked cemetery, but no trace of the mysterious Highgate Vampire was ever found.

Vampire Hunters

In vampire lore, there are many tales of brave men and women who risked their lives to rid the world of the vampire menace.

Some of the early vampire hunters were fearless avenging heroes. Others were bounty hunters who tracked down vampires for money.

Though many met a grisly fate, others survived, passing on vital vampire-fighting tactics. One hunter discovered that the Undead cannot cross running water such as a river. Another realized that a vampire cannot enter a victim's house unless invited in.

Above all else, vampire hunters needed to be well-armed and prepared. Their best bet was to catch vampires asleep during the day. Even then, it was wise to proceed with caution. A cornered vampire could lash out viciously at anyone who came near.

► *A sinister figure looms towards you out of the shadows. Is it a vampire? Run for your life!*

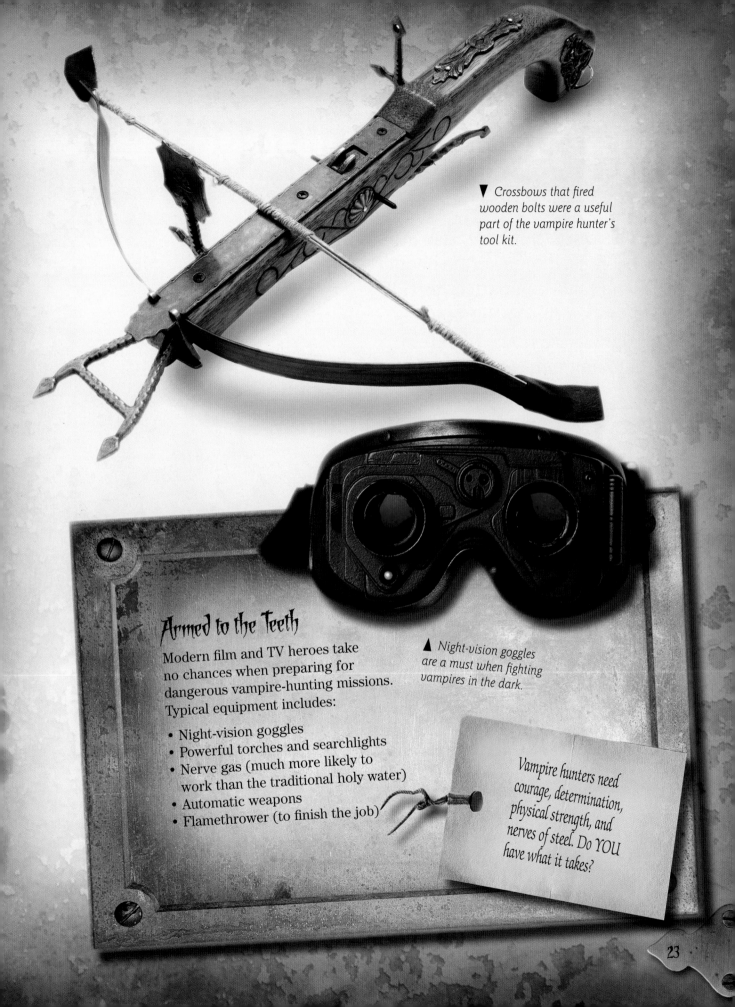

▼ Crossbows that fired wooden bolts were a useful part of the vampire hunter's tool kit.

▲ Night-vision goggles are a must when fighting vampires in the dark.

Armed to the Teeth

Modern film and TV heroes take no chances when preparing for dangerous vampire-hunting missions. Typical equipment includes:

- Night-vision goggles
- Powerful torches and searchlights
- Nerve gas (much more likely to work than the traditional holy water)
- Automatic weapons
- Flamethrower (to finish the job)

Vampire hunters need courage, determination, physical strength, and nerves of steel. Do YOU have what it takes?

Real-Life Vampires?

The word "vampire" has often been used to describe people who have committed horrific, bloody crimes. But how many were really blood-sucking monsters?

During the 1900s, Grigori Rasputin was a trusted advisor to the Russian Tsarina Alexandra. This was due to his seemingly magical ability to cure her son Alexei of a bleeding disorder called hemophilia. So Alexandra was under his spell – but why was he linked to the Undead?

The legend grew up around the story of Rasputin's death. In 1916, his body was found in the freezing Neva River. He had been shot three times, beaten and poisoned before being tied up in a rug. Even then, he almost crawled out onto the ice before finally drowning. No wonder people whispered he might still come back from the dead. But compared to Vlad Dracul (page 19) and Erzsebet Báthory (page 25), Rasputin hardly deserves the title "vampire."

▼ *Grigori Rasputin (1869 – 1916): mystic healer, scheming genius – vampire?*

"Rasputin's power came from his ability to hypnotize others. He was about six feet tall, with big grey, piercing eyes that seemed to look into your soul."

from a description by a Russian courtier

Hero or Horror?

General Gilles de Rais was a French hero in the Hundred Years War against England (1337–1453). He fought alongside Joan of Arc and, like her, was accused by his enemies of witchcraft. Under torture, he confessed to murdering dozens of boys, and to being a vampire.

The tale of Bluebeard may be based on de Rais. A rich nobleman tells his new wife she can go into any room in the castle except one. After many weeks, she cannot resist taking a peek – and finds the room full of the bloody corpses of his previous wives!

◄ *Gilles de Rais, alias Bluebeard, of France (1404–1440)*

The Blood Countess

One of the cruelest women who ever lived, the Hungarian Countess Erzsebet Báthory (1560–1614) is said to have tortured and killed dozens, if not hundreds, of young women. In legend, she bathed in their blood to keep herself looking young and beautiful. Rumors spread that Báthory was a vampire who drank her victims' blood. Both stories are probably untrue. She was just a vicious person who was powerful enough to get away with murder.

► *Erzsebet Báthory, alias the Blood Countess, of Hungary (1560–1614)*

Waking the Dead

Do you believe in vampires? In 1727, a Serbian villager called Arnod Paole broke his neck in a fall from a haywagon. Soon afterwards, strange and horrible events began to take place in the village of Medvegia. What follows is chilling – but is it fact or fiction?

▼ *The horrifying events at Medvegia aroused widespread interest. Several newspapers in England carried versions of the official report into the alleged vampire attacks.*

A few weeks after Arnod's death, local people began to complain that his corpse was stalking the village and "plaguing" them at night. Soon after, four villagers were found dead in mysterious circumstances. Panicked, the village elders summoned three officials from a nearby town to investigate. They were told that Arnod's ghost had not only murdered the victims, but had killed their cattle and sucked their blood.

Determined to end the evil, the villagers dug up Arnod's corpse. To their horror, they found his body still showed signs of life: fresh blood flowed from his eyes, nose and mouth; his old nails had fallen off and new nails had grown in their place. Convinced that Arnod was a vampire, the villagers drove a stake through his heart. As they did so, Arnod's corpse suddenly gave out a loud groan. They burned the body to ashes the same day and threw these in his grave.

▼ *In their report, the officers described what they saw when the bodies of the victims were dug up and dissected.*

"...At this, we went the same afternoon to the graveyard to investigate the graves and examine the bodies in them. After the opening of one woman's body, there was found a quantity of fresh blood. The lungs, liver and stomach were all quite fresh as they would be in a healthy person."

from the official report by two Austrian military doctors

Could the events at Medvegia be explained scientifically? Take a look at the theories below. Are YOU convinced?

Medvegia: The Theories

In the 18th century, when cases of vampires were first reported, people's knowledge of medicine was very basic. The "fresh blood" produced by Arnod's corpse could have been the reddish liquid produced when a body starts to rot. It is also common for people's nails and hair to grow after they die. The "groan" was probably caused by gases escaping from the decomposing body.

Twilight Quiz

1. You suspect one of your friends is a vampire. How would you find out?

   a Bite your lip so hard that it starts bleeding. No vampire could resist the desire to drain the blood from your body.

   b Look for telltale signs: no shadow or reflection? Suspicious blood spots on his or her clothing?

   c Offer some garlic to see if your suspect recoils in horror.

2. You're on the hunt for a vampire den in your area. Should you:

   a Wait for a dark night in the hope that you can follow one of the Undead home?

   b Search for likely haunts during the daytime when the vampires are asleep?

   c Take a look on Google Earth to see if the satellites have picked up anything suspicious.

3. A vampire has cornered you and your friend in an alley. What's your best hope of escape?

   a Try to scare off the vampire by charging at him, shouting "My granny's got sharper teeth than you!"

   b Look for anything that you could use as a weapon – such as a sharp wooden stick or something that looks like a cross.

   c Point out that your friend is a lot juicier than you and has always wanted to live forever.

4. After a desperate struggle with a vampire, you've been infected by his razor-sharp claws. Should you:

   a Get out the flamethrower? You might as well finish off every last vampire in your area before you become one of them.

   b Quickly use a tourniquet to isolate the infected area?

   c Buy a new washing machine? If you're going to be feasting on human blood every night, the laundry is going to pile up.

5. When it comes to slaying the Undead, what's your weapon of choice?

   a A wooden stake. It's messy and a lot more risky, but it's how your grandfather would have done it.

   b A crossbow with wooden bolts.

   c A rifle with telescopic sights and a clip full of silver bullets. If you take potshots from a long way off, then they won't even know it's you if you miss.

CHECK YOUR SCORE

Mostly 'a's   You're a hardcore vampire hunter, but you may not survive very long!

Mostly 'b's   You're brave but cautious – you'd get the thumbs-up from Van Helsing himself.

Mostly 'c's   Sounds like you don't have the stomach for the job. Stick to watching vampire movies from the comfort of your sofa.

Glossary

antidote cure

bacteria tiny organisms that can spread disease and infection

bounty hunter person who tracks down criminals or wrongdoers in order to claim a reward

coma a sleep-like state in which many of the body's normal functions shut down

confront to challenge or stand up to

crib a baby's bed

crypt a burial vault beneath a church

deceitful dishonest, not to be trusted

dissect to cut up carefully and examine

distract to divert someone's attention

exterminate to wipe out or destroy

fictional made-up, like a story in a book

garlic a strong-smelling plant used to flavor food

hocus-pocus nonsense or meaningless talk meant to trick people

hypnotize to put someone in a sleepy, trance-like state

hysteria a state of panic and excitement

legend a traditional story that may or may not be based on real events

locust a type of grasshopper

lore stories, customs, or beliefs passed down from one generation to the next

lure to lead someone into a trap

mesmerize to fascinate, or hold someone spellbound

myth a belief that may not be true; a traditional story, typically involving gods and goddesses or other supernatural beings

nobleman a person born into an aristocratic family

plague to pester or annoy; a serious disease that spreads quickly and affects many people

Glossary (continued)

prey to hunt and kill for food

ravenous extremely hungry

recoil to back away from

remote faraway or distant

repulsion disgust or horror

seductive attractive, hard to resist

slake to quench or satisfy

slaughter to kill

slavering dripping saliva

supernatural impossible to explain scientfically

superstition belief in something that cannot be explained scientifically

symbol a sign or token

transformation a change from one thing or state to another

tsarina title given to the wife of the tsar, the imperial ruler of Russia

virus an illness or disease that can be passed from one person to another

werewolf a person who changes into a wolf, usually at the time of the full moon

wolfsbane a wild plant with yellow or purple flowers

Further Reading and Websites

Further Reading

The Vampire Handbook, Dr. Robert Curran (A&C Black)

The Vampire Hunter's Guide, Otto De'Ath (Edge series, Franklin Watts)

Vampires, Belinda Gallagher (100 Facts series, Miles Kelly)

Vampirology, Nicky Raven (Templar)

Encyclopedia Horrifica: The Terrifying TRUTH! About Vampires, Ghosts, Monsters and More, Joshua Gee (Scholastic Books)

The Undead: Vampires, Werewolves and Zombies, Jim Pipe (Ticktock Media Ltd.)

Can Science Solve? The Mystery of Vampires and Werewolves, Chris Oxlade (Heinemann Library)

Websites

www.vampires.com
The latest news on games, stories and books about vampires.

science.howstuffworks.com/science-vs-myth/strange-creatures/vampire
Read all about the history of vampires.

www.draculas.info
Lots of gory facts on Dracula and other vampires.

http://sd4kids.skepdic.com/vampire.html/
An explanation of what scientists say about vampires and werewolves.

http://www.mythicalcreaturesguide.com/page/Vampire
This website includes vampire myths and legends from around the world.

http://zombies.monstrous.com/
Find out about how zombies began to appear in folklore and stories.

Index